fast &
Fashion Jewelry

Becky Meverden

Becky has been crafting since she was a little girl. Her motto is "I've never met a craft I didn't like!" Beading is her latest passion. She has appeared regularly on HGTV's *The Carol Duvall Show*. She is a member of the Craft and Hobby Association, The Society of Creative Designers, and the National Polymer Clay Guild. This is Becky's seventh book.

Dedication

I would like to thank the Society of Creative Designers, who have been an invaluable source of information and opportunities for me. A special thanks to the Minnesota SCD girls: Linda Wyszynski, Maureen Carlson, Nancy Hoerner—I always look forward to our breakfast meetings.

CREATE STYLISH FASHION JEWELRY THAT'S PERFECT FOR YOU! BEGINNER-FRIENDLY INSTRUCTIONS!

Now you'll always have the just-right necklace, bracelet, watch, or earrings for every outfit. Becky Meverden's fast techniques make it easy to assemble custom-fit accessories—and just imagine all the fabulous gifts you can create! Becky shares everything you need to know about clasps, wires, and findings. And you'll be amazed to discover the huge variety of beads that are available for your use. Clear instructions and stunning photography make this comprehensive jewelry guide a must-have.

LEISURE ARTS, INC.
Little Rock, AR

Basic Supplies & Tools

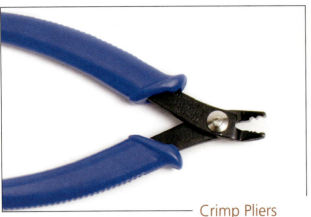

Crimp Pliers
Used with crimp
tubes or beads.

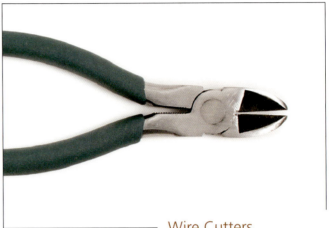

Wire Cutters
Much better than scissors
for cutting wire, headpins,
and eye pins.

Round-Nose Pliers
Used for making loops
and opening and closing
jump rings (you can also
use chain-nose or flat-
nose pliers).

Memory Wire Cutters
Used specifically to cut
memory wire. Using
regular wire cutters on
memory wire will dull and
ruin the cutters.

Flexible Beading Wire

I use this wire the most. Some well-known brands are Accu-flex®, Beadalon®, and Soft Flex®. The wire is comprised of twisted wires inside a nylon coating. The more twisted wires there are, the more flexible the beading wire. I prefer to work with 21 or 49 strands. The wire diameters range from .010" to .36". Remember, the larger and heavier the beads, the larger the wire diameter you should use. I use .015" diameter the most.

Bead Board

Great for planning a design. Lay out beads and findings in the grooved section. There are also sections for storing beads. Most bead boards have rulers on them.

Memory Wire

This is stainless steel wire that retains its coiled shape. Memory wire is very strong, so use memory wire cutters to cut it. Clasps are not needed with this wire; just loop each end to finish your design.

Beads

Celestial Crystal™ Beads
Hand-cut leaded crystal beads. These come in various colors, shapes, and sizes.

Cloisonné Beads
These handmade enameled metal beads involve multiple steps to produce.

E-beads
Same size as 6/0 beads. Also referred to as rocaille beads.

Lampwork Beads
These beads are handcrafted from rods of glass which are heated over a torch, then wrapped around mandrels.

Alphabet Beads
The beads I used are sterling silver and come in several sizes.

Pearls
Available in various shapes, sizes, and colors. Pearls add elegance to beaded projects.

Seed Beads
Available in various sizes and colors. I prefer Japanese seed beads because the beads are uniform. They are sized by number; the higher the number, the smaller the bead.

Swarovski® Crystals
Beautiful crystals made in Austria. They come in various colors, shapes, and sizes. Some of my favorite crystals are those with the aurora borealis (AB) finish, which adds a rainbow look when light shines on the crystal.

Triangle Beads
Transparent color-lined triangular beads. Available in many colors.

Bali Beads
Ornate and unique beads. They come in many sizes and shapes.

Findings

Bead Caps

Caps that cover the ends of a bead where the holes are. Make sure the bead cap is the same size as the bead. If it is a 10mm bead, the cap should be 10mm.

Crimp Tubes or Beads

Flatten these with crimp pliers to secure the ends of your design.

Ear Wires

These come in several different styles. Choose the style you like best. I used the fishhook style in this book.

Eye Pins

Straight wires with a loop at one end.

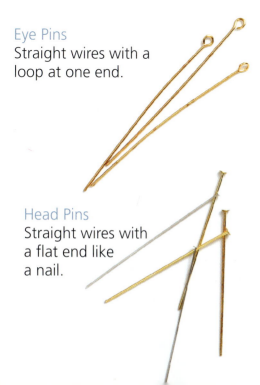

Head Pins

Straight wires with a flat end like a nail.

Jump Rings

Used in adding jewelry components such as charms or for extending the length of a design. These come in several sizes and metal types, including sterling silver.

Reducer Connectors

These reduce multiple strings into one.

Spacer Beads

Small metal beads used to accent larger beads or fill space in the design without being overly noticeable.

Toggle Clasps

These are my favorite clasps because they are so easy to incorporate in a design and are easy to fasten and unfasten.

Two-hole Spacer Bars

These prevent multiple strings from becoming tangled. They come in several sizes and metal types.

Beading Techniques

Attaching a Toggle Clasp (Crimping)
crimp tube or bead
toggle clasp
beading wire
2mm or 3mm round metal beads (optional)

1. String a crimp tube and half the clasp about 1" from the wire end. Loop the wire end back through the crimp tube. Pull the wire tight against the toggle clasp, leaving a tail.
2. Place the crimp tube into the inner notch of the crimp pliers and squeeze hard to dent the tube.
3. Place the crimp tube in the outer notch of the crimp pliers so the dent is facing the tip of the pliers; squeeze the pliers. This will fold the tube in half. Cut off the excess tail wire. Be careful not to cut the other wire.

Tip: Don't crimp your projects too tightly. This can damage beads or break the wire. To prevent this when making a necklace or bracelet, you can place the wire into the finished shape, and then add the second half of the clasp and crimp.

Tip: To add more strength, add a small, round metal bead. The stringing order will be: crimp tube, round bead, and half the clasp.

Opening & Closing a Jump Ring
1. Use 2 pairs of pliers (you can use round-, chain-, or flat-nosed pliers) to grasp the jump ring near each side of the opening. Pull one set of pliers toward you and press the other away from you to open the jump ring.
2. To close the jump ring, reverse Step 1.

Tip: Never open jump rings by pulling the ends away from each other. This will weaken and distort the jump ring.

Making an Eye Loop

1. Trim the wire to $^1/_2$".
2. Grasp the wire end with round-nose pliers. Repositioning the pliers as needed, bend the wire into a small loop; cut off any excess.
3. To open a loop, follow the instructions for opening a jump ring.

Making a Loop End on a Headpin

1. Leave at least $^1/_2$" at the top of the headpin to make the loop.
2. Grasp the headpin near the top of the last bead with round-nose pliers. Repositioning the pliers as needed, bend the wire into a small loop; cut off any excess.
3. To open a loop, follow the instructions for opening a jump ring.

Working with Sterling Silver Findings

When choosing components for a project, keep in mind that sterling silver is not inexpensive. Choose better beads to complement sterling silver findings. Remember, you are beading something that will be treasured for years to come.

Sterling silver will tarnish with time. To slow that process, I keep my sterling jewelry in plastic zipping bags.

Before You Begin

- Not sure where to find beads? If you are lucky enough to live near a bead store, it is a wonderful source. You can also find beads in many craft stores and some of the larger discount stores. How about your own jewelry box? Beads from an old necklace can be used with new beads and findings to make a stylish piece of jewelry. There are also mail order companies and Internet vendors. Another great source is on-line auctions.

- The bead colors and styles used for these projects are my choices. Feel free to substitute your favorite colors or style. Check out your favorite fashion magazine for the latest color trends. You can also find inspiration on the Internet.

- Having trouble keeping beads from rolling all over and onto the floor? When using large beads, I use a bead board. I place the beads and findings onto the bead board, arrange them to my liking, and then string them right from the board. When using small beads (seed beads), I use a Vellux® mat. I pour the beads onto the mat and string directly from the mat.

- The lengths given for the projects in this book are only a guide. For bracelets, use a measuring tape to measure the wrist; then, add 2½" to 3" to accommodate the clasp. For a necklace, I lay a measuring tape around my neck to determine the desired length and add 2½" to 3" to accommodate the clasp. When I am close to finishing the necklace, I place it around my neck to make sure it is the length I want, remembering that I still have the other half of the clasp to add.

Sources

Lampwork Beadmaker
Barley Beads
Michael Barley
Website: www.barleybeads.com
Email: beadlebarley@yahoo.com

Alphabet Beads & Charms
Charm Factory
P.O. Box 91625
Albuquerque, NM 87199-1625
Phone: 1-866-867-5266
Fax: 1-866-867-5265
Website: www.charmfactory.com
Email: sales@charmfactory.com

Beading Supplies
Fire Mountain Gems
One Fire Mountain Way
Grants Pass, OR 97526-2373
Phone: 1-800-423-2319
Fax: 1-800-292-3473
Website: www.firemountaingems.com
Email: questions@firemtn.com

Beading Supplies
Halcraft USA Inc.
60 South Macquesten Parkway
Mt. Vernon, NY 10550
Phone: 1-212-376-1580
Fax: 1-212-376-1588
Website: www.halcraft.com
Email: information@halcraft.com

Beading Supplies
Rings & Things
P.O. Box 450
Spokane, WA 99210-0450
Phone: 1-800-366-2156
Fax: 1-509-838-2602
Website: www.rings-things.com

Polymer Clay Artist
Karen "Klew" Lewis
The Spirited Bead & Klew's Gallery
435 West J Street
Tehachapi, CA 93561
Phone & Fax: 1-661-823-1930
Website: www.klewexpressions.com
Email: klew@klewexpressions.com

Birthstone Bracelet

.015" diameter nylon-coated stainless steel beading wire
2 silver crimp tubes
2 – 3mm silver disc beads
silver heart toggle clasp
6 – 6mm silver heart beads
3mm silver beads
2 – 10mm 2-hole silver spacer bars
4mm cream pearls
8 – 6mm Swarovski® bicone beads (4 for the birthstone color of each person)
4 – 6mm silver granulated Bali spacer beads
6mm sterling silver alphabet beads
Basic Supplies shown on pages 2-3

Finished length: 9"

Crystal Birthstone Chart	
January	Garnet
February	Amethyst
March	Aquamarine
April	Crystal
May	Emerald
June	Light Amethyst
July	Ruby
August	Peridot
September	Sapphire
October	Rose
November	Topaz
December	Blue Zircon

Read Beading Basics on pages 2-8 before beginning. If one name is longer than the other, arrange the beads on a bead board or piece of felt to center the names on the bracelet. Adjust the amount of pearls on each end as needed.

1. Cut two 11" wire lengths. String a crimp tube, a disc bead, and half the clasp onto both wires; crimp.
2. String both wires through a heart bead. Separate the wires and string the following onto each: a silver bead, spacer bar (string onto both wire ends), 3 pearls, and a silver bead. Repeat the pearls and silver bead sequence adjusting for the length of the names. At the middle of each wire, string a bicone bead, heart bead, bicone bead, spacer bead, the name in alphabet beads, spacer bead, bicone bead, heart bead, bicone bead, silver bead, and 3 pearls. Repeat the length as you did on the other side.
3. String a spacer bar and 2 silver beads. Bring the wire ends together and thread them through a heart bead. String a crimp tube, a disc bead, and the other half of the clasp onto both wires; crimp.

Turquoise

Necklace

.015" diameter nylon-coated
   stainless steel beading wire
2 silver crimp tubes
silver heart toggle clasp
tape
144 – 3mm black E beads
23 – 9mm round turquoise beads
264 – 8/0 seed beads (turquoise
   assortment)
20 – 11mm flat oval turquoise
   beads
19 – 10mm black faceted beads
19 – 11mm turquoise faceted
   oval beads
Basic Supplies shown on
   pages 2-3

Finished length: 26"

*Read Beading Basics on
pages 2-8 before beginning.*

1. Cut three 30" wire lengths.
   String a crimp tube and half
   the clasp onto one end of all 3
   wires; crimp.
2. Tape the clasp and wires to a
   flat surface for stability while
   beading.
3. On wire #1 (it doesn't matter
   which wire), string 6 E beads,
   a round turquoise bead, 6 E
   beads, and a second round
   turquoise bead. String 22 seed
   beads onto wire #2, and then
   string the wire through the
   second round turquoise bead
   on wire #1 (Fig. 1). Separate
   the wires and repeat the above
   sequence 10 more times. On
   wire #1, string 6 E beads, a
   round turquoise bead, and 6
   E beads. On wire #2, string 22
   seed beads. Tape down wires
   #1 and #2.

4. On wire #3, string 2 flat oval
   beads, a black faceted bead,
   2 turquoise faceted beads, and
   a black faceted bead. Repeat
   this sequence 8 more times.
   String 2 flat oval beads, a black
   faceted bead, and a turquoise
   faceted bead.
5. Thread wire #3 up and down
   through the openings left by
   the other wires. It will look
   braided. Remove the tape from
   all wires.
6. String a crimp tube and the
   other half of the clasp onto the
   end of all 3 wires; crimp.

Fig. 1

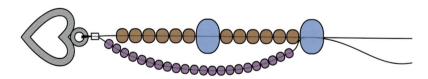

Bali Earrings

2 – 3mm round silver beads
2 – 12mm Bali saucer beads
2 – 16mm Bali saucer beads
 (random triangles all over bead)
2 – 10mm granulated Bali beads
2 – 2" silver headpins
2 silver ear wires
Basic Supplies shown on pages 2-3

*Read Beading Basics on pages 2-8
before beginning.*

For each earring, string a 3mm
bead, 12mm bead, 16mm bead,
and 10mm bead onto a headpin.
Use round-nose pliers to make
a small loop in the pin end and
attach the pin to an ear wire. Trim
the excess wire.

Pearl Necklace

.015" diameter nylon-coated stainless steel beading wire
2 silver crimp tubes
24 – 3mm round silver beads
silver toggle clasp
tape
110 – 3mm pearl E beads
10 – 10mm silver Bali beads
252 – 11/0 transparent white seed beads
54 – 6mm silver daisy spacer beads
18 – 10mm pearls
9 – 15mm silver flat oval Bali beads
Basic Supplies shown on pages 2-3

Finished length: $17^1/_2$"

Read Beading Basics on pages 2-8 before beginning.

1. Cut three 20" wire lengths. String a crimp tube, 3mm round silver bead, and half the clasp onto the 3 wire ends; crimp.
2. Tape the clasp and wires to a flat surface for stability while beading.
3. On wire #1 (it doesn't matter which wire), string 10 E beads and a 10mm Bali bead. Repeat this sequence 9 more times. String 10 more E beads and tape down the end.
4. On wire #2, string a 3mm round silver bead and 12 seed beads. Repeat this sequence 20 more times. String another 3mm round silver bead and tape down the end.
5. On wire #3, string 2 daisy spacers, a 10mm pearl, 2 daisy spacers, a 10mm pearl, 2 daisy spacers, and a flat oval bead. Repeat this sequence 8 more times. Remove the tape from all wires.
6. String a crimp tube, a 3mm silver bead, and the other half of the clasp onto all 3 wires; crimp.

Amber &

Gold Bracelet

Gold Earrings

3 loops of bracelet memory wire
21 – 8mm gold aurora borealis (AB)
  Celestial Crystal™ beads
11 – 8mm amber Czech fire polished
  faceted rounds
59 amber silver-lined triangle beads
2" silver headpin
2 – 3mm gold disc beads
2 – gold bead caps
2 – 6mm gold daisy spacers
Basic Supplies shown on pages 2-3

*Read Beading Basics on pages 2-8
before beginning.*

Use round-nose pliers to make a small
eye loop in one wire end. String a
gold AB bead, Czech bead, gold AB
bead, and 6 triangle beads. Repeat
this sequence 9 more times, stringing
only 5 triangle beads on the last set.
Use round-nose pliers to form a small
loop in the wire end. On the headpin,
string a disc bead, bead cap, Czech
bead, bead cap, disc bead, daisy
spacer, gold AB bead, and another
daisy spacer. Use round-nose pliers to
bend the pin end into a loop. Thread
the loop through one of the memory
wire end loops. Tighten the loop on
the pin and cut off the excess wire.

8 – 6mm gold daisy spacers
4 – 8mm amber Czech fire-polished faceted rounds
24 silver-lined amber triangle beads
6 – 2" gold headpins
2 – 3-strand gold reducer connectors
2 – 4mm gold beads
2 – 8mm gold aurora borealis (AB) Celestial Crystal™ beads
2 gold ear wires
Basic Supplies shown on pages 2-3

Read Beading Basics on pages 2-8 before beginning.

1. For each earring, string a daisy spacer, Czech bead,
   another daisy spacer, and 4 triangle beads onto a
   headpin. Use round-nose pliers to make a loop in the
   pin end, attaching the pin to the first loop on one
   connector. Trim the excess wire.
2. String a 4mm bead, 2 triangle beads, AB bead, and 2
   triangle beads onto a headpin. Use round-nose pliers
   to make a loop in the pin end, attaching the pin to the
   center loop on the connector. Trim the excess wire.
3. String a daisy spacer, 4 triangle beads, another daisy
   spacer, and a Czech bead onto a headpin. Use round-
   nose pliers to make a loop in the pin end, attaching the
   pin to the third loop on the connector.
4. Use round-nose pliers to attach the connector to an
   ear wire.

Spoon Bracelet
with Violet Dangle

Pink & Green Option

2 sterling silver spoons
fine-point permanent marker
small fabric scrap
vise
hacksaw
steel file
drill with $1/16$" metal drill bit
metal pipe the diameter of
    your wrist
rubber mallet
7mm silver jump rings
silver heart toggle clasp
17mm silver filigree heart
    charm
2mm round silver bead
3 – 5mm silver daisy spacer
    beads
6mm Swarovski® violet bicone
    bead
6mm Swarovski® crystal aurora
    borealis (AB) bicone bead
2" headpin
Basic Supplies shown on
    pages 2-3

*Read Beading Basics on pages
2-8 before beginning.*

1. For each spoon, measure
   around your wrist; divide
   by 2. Measure this distance
   from the handle end and
   use the marker to mark the
   cutting line on the back of
   the spoon. Wrap the fabric
   scrap around the spoon
   handle above the cutting
   line. Place the handle in the
   vise and tighten. Saw along
   the cutting line.

2. File the rough edges
   smooth.
3. Drill a hole $1/8$" from each
   end of the spoon.
4. Cover each piece with
   the fabric scrap, place the
   spoon handle against the
   pipe, and use the rubber
   mallet to bend it to fit
   around half of the wrist.
   Bend the other spoon
   handle to match.
5. Connect the handles at the
   wide end with a jump ring.
6. Attach a jump ring and half
   the clasp to each narrow
   handle end. If the spoon
   pieces aren't long enough,
   add extra jump rings to the
   narrow ends to lengthen
   the bracelet.
7. Use a jump ring to attach
   the heart charm to the
   center jump ring on the
   bracelet front.
8. String a 2mm bead, daisy
   spacer, violet bicone bead,
   daisy spacer, crystal bicone
   bead, and another daisy
   spacer onto the headpin.
   Use round-nose pliers to
   make a small loop in the pin
   end and attach the pin to
   the center jump ring.

2 sterling silver spoons
fine-point permanent marker
small fabric scrap
vise
hacksaw
steel file
drill with $1/16$" metal drill bit
metal pipe the diameter of your wrist
rubber mallet
7mm silver jump rings
silver heart toggle clasp
14mm silver heart charm
2mm round silver bead
6 – 5mm silver daisy spacer beads
6mm Swarovski® light rose aurora
    borealis (AB) bicone bead
6mm Swarovski® chrysolite (AB) bicone
    bead
2" headpin
Basic Supplies shown on pages 2-3

*Read Beading Basics on pages 2-8
before beginning.*

1. Follow Steps 1-7 of the Spoon
   Bracelet with Violet Dangle.
2. String a 2mm bead, 2 daisy spacers,
   light rose bicone bead, 2 daisy
   spacers, chrysolite bicone bead, and
   2 daisy spacers onto the headpin.
   Use round-nose pliers to make a
   small loop in the pin end and attach
   the pin to the center jump ring on
   the bracelet front.

Cloisonné Necklace

.015" diameter nylon-coated
    stainless steel beading wire
2 gold crimp tubes
12 – 2mm gold beads
gold toggle clasp
22 – 6mm gold daisy spacer beads
60 – 11/0 light blue seed beads
10 – 6mm Swarovski® jonquil
    aurora borealis (AB) bicone
    beads
60 – 11/0 gold lined transparent
    white seed beads
6 – 13mm blue floral cloisonné
    disc beads
5 – 8mm Swarovski® light sapphire
    bicone beads
Basic Supplies shown on pages 2-3

Finished length: 17"

Read Beading Basics on pages 2-8 before beginning.

1. Cut a 20" wire length. String a crimp tube, 2mm gold bead, and half the clasp on one end; crimp.
2. String a daisy spacer, 10 light blue beads, daisy spacer, jonquil bead, daisy spacer, 10 white beads, daisy spacer, and a jonquil bead. Repeat once.
3. String a daisy spacer, 10 light blue beads, daisy spacer, jonquil bead, daisy spacer, and 10 white beads.
4. String a cloisonné bead, 2mm gold bead, light sapphire bead, and a 2mm gold bead. Repeat this sequence 4 more times. String the last cloisonné bead.
5. String 10 white beads, a daisy spacer, jonquil bead, daisy spacer, 10 light blue beads, daisy spacer, jonquil bead, and a daisy spacer; repeat once.
6. String 10 white beads, a daisy spacer, jonquil bead, daisy spacer, 10 light blue beads, and a daisy spacer.
7. String a crimp tube, 2mm gold bead, and the other half of the clasp; crimp.

.015" diameter nylon-coated
   stainless steel beading wire
2 silver crimp tubes
silver toggle clasp
42 – 6mm silver daisy spacer beads
76 – 3mm pearl E beads
21 – 8mm light blue iridescent
   teardrop beads
3mm round silver bead
2" headpin
Basic Supplies shown on pages 2-3

Finished length: 17³/₄"

Read Beading Basics on pages 2-8 before beginning.

1. Cut a 21" wire length. String a crimp tube and half the clasp onto one wire end; crimp.
2. String a daisy spacer, 4 E beads, a daisy spacer, and a teardrop bead. Repeat this sequence 17 more times.
3. String a daisy spacer, 4 E beads, and a daisy spacer.
4. String a crimp tube and the other half of the clasp onto the wire end; crimp.
5. String a round silver bead, daisy spacer, and a teardrop bead onto the headpin. Repeat the spacer and teardrop 2 more times and string another daisy spacer.
6. Use round-nose pliers to make a loop in the headpin and attach it to the center of the necklace (in the middle of the tenth set of E beads). Close the loop tightly.

Earth Tone Necklace

.015" diameter nylon-coated
  stainless steel beading wire
4 gold crimp tubes
2 – 1" eyepins
tape
11/0 seed beads (earth tone
  assortment)
8 – 6mm red agate round beads
2 – 5/8" gold cones
2 – 6mm gold jump rings
gold toggle clasp
40mm leopard skin jasper donut
Basic Supplies shown on pages 2-3

Finished length: 24"

*Read Beading Basics on pages 2-8
before beginning.*

1. Cut three 29½" and two 19½"
   lengths of beading wire. String
   a crimp tube onto one end of
   all three 29½" wires. Thread
   the ends through an eyepin
   and crimp (Fig. 1).
2. String a crimp tube onto one
   end of both 19½" lengths.
   Thread the ends through the
   same eyepin and crimp (Fig. 1).

Fig. 1

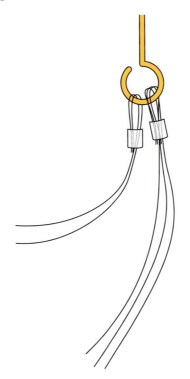

3. Tape the eyepin and wires to a
   flat surface for stability while
   beading. String 27½" of each
   29½" length with seed beads.
   String 17½" of each 19½"
   length with seed beads, adding
   agate beads to each strand
   (make sure the agates don't
   line up next to each other).
4. String a crimp tube onto the
   remaining end of all three
   29½" wires. Thread the ends
   through the remaining eyepin
   and crimp. Repeat with the
   19½" lengths.
5. String a cone onto each eyepin.
   Use round-nose pliers to make
   a loop in the eyepin end.
6. Use a jump ring to attach a
   clasp half to each eyepin.
7. Hold the ends together to find
   the center of the long strands.
   Pull the center loop through the
   donut. Slip all the strands down
   through the loop and gently
   pull to tighten.

Sapphire Necklace

.015" diameter nylon-coated
   stainless steel beading wire
10 – 6mm silver granulated Bali
   spacer beads
2 silver crimp tubes
2 – 4mm silver disc beads
silver toggle clasp
240 E beads (colors to match the
   focal bead)
6 – 10mm 2-hole silver spacer bars
2 – 9mm silver granulated Bali
   spacer beads
28mm lampwork focal bead (This
   one was made by Jim Barley.)
Basic Supplies shown on pages 2-3

Finished length: 23"

Read Beading Basics on pages 2-8 before beginning.

1. Cut two 26" wire lengths. String a crimp tube, a 4mm disc bead, and half the clasp onto one end of both wires; crimp. String a 6mm spacer bead.
2. String 10 E beads and a 6mm spacer bead onto both wires. Repeat this sequence 3 more times.
3. Following Fig. 1, separate the wires and string 10 E beads onto each wire and a spacer bar onto both wires. Repeat this sequence 2 more times. String 10 more E beads on each wire.
4. String a 9mm spacer bead, the focal bead, and another 9mm spacer bead onto both wires.
5. Repeat Step 3. String a 6mm spacer bead onto both wires.
6. Repeat Step 2.
7. String a crimp tube, 4mm disc bead, and the other half of the clasp onto both wires; crimp.

Fig. 1

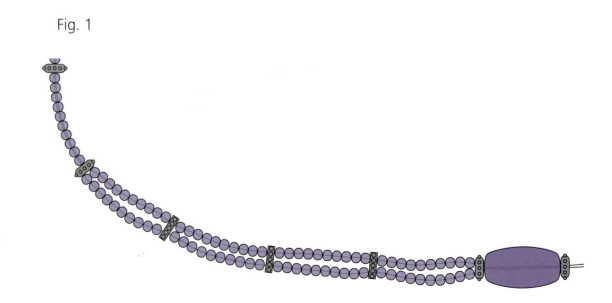

Green Earrings

6 – 7mm silver spacer beads (fan-like)
2 – 12mm green/clear cylinder beads
6 – 8/0 seed beads (similar in color to the cylinder beads)
2 – 2" silver headpins
2 silver ear wires
Basic Supplies shown on pages 2-3

Read Beading Basics on pages 2-8 before beginning.

For each earring, string a spacer bead, cylinder bead, spacer bead, 3 seed beads, and another spacer bead onto a headpin. Use round-nose pliers to make a small loop in the pin end and attach the pin to an ear wire. Trim the excess wire.

.020" diameter nylon-coated
stainless steel beading wire
2 silver crimp tubes
2 – 2mm round silver beads
silver toggle clasp
2 – 4mm silver daisy spacers
2 – 5mm silver Bali beads
10 – 4mm silver wire-centered
Bali spacer beads
12 – 4mm silver ruffle-edged Bali
spacer beads
8 – 4mm silver granulated Bali
spacer beads
6 – 6mm silver granulated Bali
beads
4 – 10mm silver Bali beads
Basic Supplies shown on pages 2-3

Finished length: 7¼"

*Read Beading Basics on pages 2-8
before beginning.*

1. Cut a 10" wire length. String
   a crimp tube, 2mm bead, and
   half the clasp onto one end;
   crimp.
2. String a daisy spacer, 5mm Bali
   bead, 5 wire-centered spacers,
   6 ruffle-edged spacers, 4mm
   granulated spacer, and a 6mm
   Bali bead. Repeat the last 2
   beads twice more.
3. String a 4mm granulated
   spacer, four 10mm Bali beads,
   3 sets of a 4mm granulated
   spacer and 6mm Bali bead,
   a 4 mm granulated spacer,
   6 ruffle-edged spacers,
   5 wire-centered spacers,
   a 5mm Bali bead, and a daisy
   spacer.
4. String a crimp tube, a 2mm
   bead, and the other half of the
   clasp; crimp.

Turquoise Earrings

6 – 2mm round silver beads
6 – 5mm silver daisy spacer beads
56 – 8/0 seed beads (turquoise assortment)
6 – 2" silver headpins
2 turquoise drops with three loops on one side
2 silver ear wires
Basic Supplies shown on pages 2-3

Read Beading Basics on pages 2-8 before beginning.

1. For each of the 2 outer dangles of each earring, string a 2mm bead, a daisy spacer, and 8 seed beads onto a headpin. Use round-nose pliers to make a small loop in the pin ends. Attach the dangles to the outer loops on the turquoise drop. Trim the excess wire.
2. For each center dangle, repeat Step 1, using 12 seed beads and attaching the dangle to the center loop on the drop.
3. Attach each drop to an ear wire.

3 loops of bracelet memory wire
24 – 7mm coiled silver spacer beads
12 – 10mm square turquoise beads
8/0 frosted brown seed beads
3mm round silver bead
9mm silver square Bali bead
2" silver headpin
Basic Supplies shown on pages 2-3

Read Beading Basics on pages 2-8 before beginning.

1. Use round-nose pliers to make a small eye loop in one wire end. String a spacer bead, turquoise bead, spacer bead, and 14 seed beads. Repeat this pattern, varying the amount of seed beads (I used 8, 10, or 16). Stop about $3/8$" from the end and use the pliers to form a small eye loop.
2. String the round silver bead, a spacer bead, turquoise bead, spacer bead, and the square Bali bead onto the headpin. Use round-nose pliers to bend the pin end into a loop. Attach the pin to the memory wire end loop. Tighten the loop on the pin and cut off the excess wire.

Silver Watch

.015" diameter nylon-coated,
  stainless steel beading wire
silver watch face
4 – 12mm silver Bali disc beads
8 – 7mm coiled silver spacer beads
4 – 8mm Swarovski® crystal aurora
  borealis (AB) bicone beads
2 – 9mm silver Bali beads
2 – silver crimp tubes
silver star toggle clasp
Basic Supplies shown on pages 2-3

Finished length: 8¼"

*Read Beading Basics on pages 2-8
before beginning.*

1. Cut two 8" wire lengths.
2. For each side, thread one wire
   length through the hole on one
   side of the watch face until the
   ends are even.
3. Bring both wire ends together
   and string a disc bead, spacer
   bead, AB bead, spacer bead,
   9mm bead, spacer bead, AB
   bead, spacer bead, and a disc
   bead.
4. String a crimp tube and half the
   clasp; crimp.

.015" diameter nylon-coated, stainless steel beading wire

copper watch face

4 – 8mm Swarovski® light Colorado topaz bicone beads

8 – 10mm 2-hole copper spacer bars

12 – 12mm unakite twisted oval beads

4 – 4mm Swarovski® light Colorado topaz round beads

2 gold crimp tubes

copper toggle clasp

Basic Supplies shown on pages 2-3

Finished length: 7¼"

Read Beading Basics on pages 2-8 before beginning.

1. Cut two 7" wire lengths.
2. For each side, thread one wire length through the holes in one side of the watch face until the ends are even.
3. String the following onto each wire end: a bicone bead, spacer bar (string onto both wire ends), and a unakite bead. Repeat this sequence 2 more times with the spacer bars and unakite beads only.
4. String a spacer bar onto both wire ends. String a round bead onto each end.
5. Bring the wire ends together. String a crimp tube and half the clasp; crimp.

Watch Tips

Make sure the watch works properly. It would be a shame to put the time and effort into stringing a gorgeous beaded watch only to discover that the watch doesn't work.

Watch faces range from inexpensive to expensive. The same can be said for beads and findings. For a nicer look, be sure your watch face, beads, and findings are of equal quality.

Discover the creative world of **Leisure Arts** publications, where inspiration lives on every page.

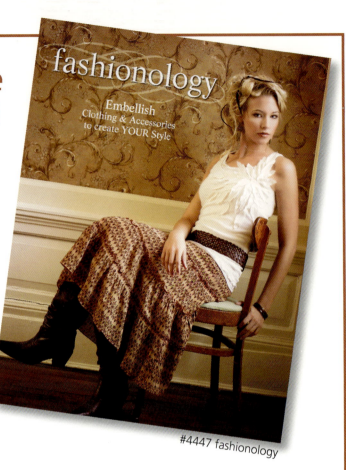

#4447 fashionology

Your next great idea starts here.